A HAIKU MENAGERIE

A HAIKU MENAGERIE

LIVING CREATURES
IN POEMS AND PRINTS

By Stephen Addiss

with Fumiko
and Akira Yamamoto

BOSTON WEATHERHILL LONDON

WEATHERHILL
an imprint of Shambhala Publications, Inc.
Horticultural Hall
300 Massachusetts Avenue
Boston, Massachusetts 02115
www.shambhala.com

First edition, 1992
Fifth printing, 2005

Printed in China
⊗ This edition is printed on acid-free paper that meets the
American National Standards Institute Z39.48 Standard.
Distributed in the United States by Random House, Inc.,
and in Canada by Random House of Canada Ltd

Library of Congress Cataloging-in-Publication Data

A Haiku menagerie: living creatures in poems and prints /
[edited] by Stephen Addiss with Fumiko and Akira
Yamamoto.—1st ed.
p. cm.
English and Japanese.
ISBN 0-8348-0248-1
ISBN 0-8348-0569-3 (2nd ed.)
1. Haiku—Translations into English. 2. Animals—Poetry.
I. Addiss, Stephen, 1935– II. Yamamoto, Fumiko
III. Yamamoto, Akira
PL782.E8H34 1992
895.6'104—dc20
92-18921
CIP

CONTENTS

Walkers, Flyers, Crawlers, Swimmers

For most of human history, people have lived in close contact with other living creatures. In the modern world, however, more and more of us are encased in concrete jungles, cut off from the natural world. As we lose contact with other living beings, we are in danger of feeling ourselves alone in the universe; the arts of poetry and painting can help us to awaken to our interrelationships with everything that lives.

The earliest of Japanese writings reveal a world where humans and animals exist side-by-side. Many creatures shared the mythological cosmos with both deities and humans, as described in the *Kojiki* (*Record of Ancient Matters*, 712) and the *Nihongi* (*Chronicles of Japan*, 720). These records tell of the importance of beasts, fowls, fish and insects to the ancient Japanese, whose world view was anthropomorphic. Some creatures in mythology were frightening and dangerous, such as the famous Yamata no Orochi, a ravenous eight-forked serpent with red glaring eyes who devoured seven maidens before he was subdued. But since the time of these ancient records, all life forms—animals on land and fish in the sea, insects, bugs, and scaly crawlers—have also played an important role in the aesthetic sensibility of the Japanese.

The introduction of Buddhism gave new impetus to the Japanese respect for all living creatures. In stories of former lives of the Buddha (the Jataka tales), the Buddha was born and performed meritorious acts in the forms of animals, while in other religious texts animals were major actors in the drama of salvation. The importance of all living creatures in Japanese art became especially notable during the Heian period (794–1185). Artistic motifs of living beings decorated objects made for use as offerings to Shinto as well as Buddhist deities. The same motifs were also utilized in secular arts, such as the beautifully decorated papers upon which poets and calligraphers wrote their selections of Chinese and Japanese poems.

The classic Japanese five-line *waka* poems of thirty-one syllables (5-7-5-7-7) have usually depicted natural scenes, often including living creatures. *Waka* poets, most of whom were from the upper echelons of society, were highly sensitive to the cyclical changes of nature. In addition to adopting from China creatures long associated with special meanings—such as the auspicious crane and tortoise—Japanese poets incorporated creatures familiar and dear from their native surroundings. *Waka* poets' awareness of the passing of time, partially influenced by the Buddhist idea of impermanence, often led to pensive verses. The passing of the seasons formed a cycle, and the ebb and flow of life reminded poets of their own mortality.

> In the summer mountains
> on the leafy treetops
> the cuckoo sings—
> and echoing back from afar
> comes his distant voice
>> *Otomo no Yakamochi*

Only a limited cast of creatures appeared in *waka*, however, and most were linked with a season. Warblers in the spring, cuckoos in summer, and deer in fall were favored as embodiments of the poets' emotions. This limitation in scope provided focus and intensity, but it eventually led to the codification and decline of the classical poetic tradition. In the long course of the history of *waka*, the creatures and natural phenomena that once communicated genuine emotions lost their vitality and were reduced to stock poetic devices.

It was in three-line haiku poems of 5-7-5 syllables that living creatures, big and small, regained their vitality. Haiku, emerging from linked verse (*haiku no renga*) was a commoners' poetic expression. The *hai* in haiku (originally called *haikai*) means to deviate from the traditional and the ordinary, to be light-hearted—in contrast to the refined spirit of *waka*. Early *haikai* tended to be frivolous, but the poetic form found its vibrant spirit in the seventeenth century when Matsuo Bashō set his gaze on nature and the living creatures around him. In his poems he captured the meeting between the universal pulse of nature and the intensely human aesthetic perception of a particular time and space.

Bashō and his followers concentrated on our immediate environment, in which humble creatures who had no place in lofty *waka* appeared as protagonists. A spider scurries up the wall as fast as it can:

> Lightening!
> fleeing up the wall,
> the legs of a spider
> *Kichō*

In the poet's eyes, the flash of lightning and the darting of the spider's legs are juxtaposed. It is a fresh awakening to the existence of other living creatures and their power to stimulate the human artistic spirit.

The eighteenth-century poet-painter Yosa Buson was another haiku master whose vision captured a tiny but vibrant insects' realm, a realm too modest for *waka* poets to extol:

> After a short night,
> on a hairy caterpillar—
> pearls of dew

In one sense this is the unique vision of a great artist, but it also represents an understanding and respect for all living beings. Humans are not regarded as controlling the forces of nature; rather, they are in harmony with them. Another haiku poet expressed amusement at the shared rhythm of mankind and other living creatures:

> Reed warblers
> follow the same beats
> as the boat maker
> *Sōtan*

It is true that in haiku natural phenomena are conventionally associated with seasonal changes, just as they were in *waka*. But haiku poets also entrusted their personal feelings to the living beings of the natural world. For example, Bashō expressed his melancholy to his friends on the verge of departing for a long journey to the north:

> Spring is passing—
> birds cry out, and there are tears
> in the eyes of the fish

Haiku masters established personal relationships with the natural world. According to folk beliefs, the frog was a messenger of the deity of rice fields. But in a poem by the haiku master Issa, the frog casts off its mythical robe:

> Challenging me
> to a staring game—
> a giant frog

Here the poet's view is still anthropocentric, but the relationship between him and the frog does not allow human sentiment to override animal existence. It is instead a personification, in which creatures and humans become fellow members of the same world, with equal rights. Empathy is perfected.

The artists who designed wood-block prints responded to the haiku animal world. The living creatures in these books romp, climb, and swim according to their own natures. Yet they approach us with tremendous openness, conveying our interconnections with them and with all beings on earth. Haiku poets and woodblock artists continue to invite us to join them in their special recognition of the immensely fascinating and delightful utopia of all living creatures.

Japanese Woodblock Books

Woodblock printed books of the Edo and Meiji periods (1600–1912) are the greatest hidden treasures of Japanese art. Although single-sheet prints of the Ukiyo-e school have achieved a worldwide reputation, the prints created for woodblock books, representing many other schools of art, remain almost unknown. Yet they fully express the manifold skills of artists, engravers, and woodblock printers, and include some of the most delightful works in all East Asian visual culture. This volume offers a selection of the most eloquent and evocative designs of living creatures by many of the finest artists of traditional Japan.

Why should woodblock books be so obscure? There are a few splendid private and public collections in the Western world, but only recently have scholars, librarians, and curators discovered their quality and variety; very few exhibitions have been available for the public. In Japan, interest has been even slower to develop. This may be because books are modest in size, and they have traditionally been considered separate from "art" when it is defined as paintings and single-sheet prints. But the prints in woodblock books were made in exactly the same fashion as individual ukiyo-e prints, the only practical difference being that they were sewn together in books. They are, in effect, woodblock-print series in bound form.

In order to understand the artistic values of Japanese woodblock books, a glimpse into their history may be useful. Until the sixteenth century, woodblock printing was utilized almost exclusively for Buddhist images and texts for the devout. Secular books were limited to the aristocracy and the clergy; because of the small number of books needed, texts were copied by hand. In the late sixteenth century, however, a new type of printing was introduced that would have a tremendous impact upon the course of Japanese publishing and, consequently, book illustration. Movable type was introduced both from Europe (a Jesuit mission brought a printing press to Japan in 1582) and from Korea, where it had long been known. This method or printing, however, was cumbersome for the Japanese language, with its tens of thousands of graphs for words and syllables. Whether type faces were made of wood, metal, or ceramic, the process of maintaining and setting so many different graphs was extremely costly. Nevertheless, the introduction of movable type was important in stimulating the publishing industry, and between 1590 and 1650 a number of beautifully printed and illustrated secular books were prepared for an exclusive clientele.

In 1600, Japan came to the end of a long period of civil wars. In the ensuing era of peace and prosperity, known as the Edo period, literacy among the general populace began to increase dramatically, and larger quantities of books were needed than ever before. The artistic capital of Kyoto was the first important center for printing, and by 1635 a wide range of books including classical and modern literature, how-to books, and scholarly volumes was being printed. Publishers in the new political capital of Edo (Tokyo) were at first branches of Kyoto firms, but by the late seventeenth century Edo became the most important center for publishing in Japan, as large numbers of newly affluent townsmen discovered the pleasures of woodblock books.

After 1650, the use of movable type was almost completely abandoned in favor of the more economical method of single-block printing, in which complete pages of text and illustrations could be carved and printed from a single board. The pictures and the words were carved in exactly the same manner on the same wooden surface, and this method had important implications for art. Because the actual process of carving permitted any juxtaposition of text and images, artists could combine or alternate words and pictures with complete design freedom. There was no difference in medium between image and text, allowing every variety of interplay between the two. As a result of the ensuing creativity of both authors and artists, woodblock books became increasingly popular. Their audience eventually became almost the total populace of Edo-period Japan. Not only did a large percentage of people learn to read, at least mastering the Japanese *kana* syllabary and a limited number of Chinese characters, but even children and adults who were not literate could enjoy the illustrated woodblock books by masters of the many different artistic schools that flourished in the Edo period.

Woodblock books became so popular that they were often copied and printed by clandestine publishers in illegal pirate editions. Partly for this reason, publisher's associations roughly equivalent to guilds were formed to try to control printing and distribution. The production process consisted of scribes *(hikkō)* to prepare the texts in elegant calligraphy prior to carving, artists *(gakka)* to supply drawings for the illustrations, engravers *(hori)* to carve the blocks, and printers *(suri)* to ink the blocks, prepare and place the paper upon them, and rub the back of the paper with barens. The publisher was in charge of the entire production, and he was also responsible for sales. Books were not only available in stores, but also from street vendors in both cities and countryside. For those who could not afford to purchase books, by the middle of the Edo period there were more than eight hundred public lending libraries in Edo alone, and peddlers would rent as well as sell books to their clients. Publishing flourished phenomenally. During the first decades of the seventeenth century, it is estimated that no more than one hundred or two hundred copies of each book were published. In contrast, by the early nineteenth century, works of popular fiction were printed in editions of ten thousand and fifteen thousand. There was a printing explosion: more than one hundred thousand different titles were published between 1600 and the close of the Edo period in 1868.

It is commonly believed that books became popular as an inexpensive medium through which to enjoy poetry, prose, and visual art, but the early books were not designed for the mass market. A typical volume of the early seventeenth century featured high-quality paper, lavish illustrations, elaborate covers, and a classical text. Its audience was the lesser nobility and wealthy educated merchants. The market for woodblock books, however, soon expanded. By the late eighteenth century, for example, large numbers of small-format, popular books (called *kibyoshi* for their yellow covers) were cheaply printed. Telling romantic stories of life in the pleasure quarters, they included many small illustrations, almost like comic books, and were written for the semi-literate townspeople. By this time the variety of books being published was astonishing. Everything from Confucian philosophy to cooking manuals, from compendiums of art to instructions on flower arranging, and from encyclopedias to pornography, found a ready market. For the first time in Japanese history, books appealed to every class, and art was a vital element in most forms of publishing.

The development of color printing is a complex story. A few early Buddhist prints used color, such as a section of the *Diamond Sutra* that was printed in 1340 with both red and black inks on a single block, giving it a talismanic quality. Yet printed color in woodblock books did not appear in Japan until the second quarter of the seventeenth century. Single-sheet prints did not utilize printed color until the 1740s, and did not feature a complete palette until the extremely popular "brocade" prints of Suzuki Harunobu of the 1760s. Although it was slow to evolve, the technique of carving separate blocks for each color eventually won favor for both books and single-sheet prints because this method permitted controlled application of different tints and hues.

Throughout their history, Japanese woodblock books have utilized color only at certain times and for certain effects. When depicting a multi-hued kimono, or adding flowering blossoms or autumn leaves to a landscape, color can be essential. In this volume about living creatures, color is a crucial factor in displaying the proud plumage of a rooster, or the rich brown body of a deer. Nevertheless, the integrity of black-and-white printing was never lost, as shown here in the swirling shape of an octopus or the bold gesture of a crow. It is no coincidence that most of the illustrations chosen for this volume were originally printed only with ink. As East Asian artists have known for many hundreds of years, black on white can sometimes enhance the sense of line, shape, and form more than the brightest tints and hues.

Japanese single-sheet prints were produced almost entirely by artists of the Ukiyo-e school, portraying the "floating world" of the entertainment districts. Individual prints could be hung in frames, mounted on scrolls, or simply attached to the walls. The subjects for these prints were usually the heroes and heroines of urban culture: swashbuckling Kabuki actors and beautiful courtesans, although in the nineteenth century a burgeoning interest in landscape was effectively explored by Katsushika Hokusai and Andō Hiroshige.

In contrast, as mentioned earlier, the designs for woodblock prints published in books were created by artists of many different schools, and they served as a more intimate entertainment for many levels of society while portraying a wide variety of subjects. Figures of all kinds; landscapes in Chinese as well as Japanese styles; flowers, plants, and trees; scenes of everyday life in the cities and countryside; Buddhist themes; specialized subjects ranging from clothing design to the ten stages of pregnancy; and all living creatures of air, land, and sea. In effect, a microcosm of Edo-period painting subjects can be seen in these books, with masters from every major tradition represented.

Most of the prints that appear in woodblock books were designed for that purpose and format; publishers regularly commissioned leading artists to design or contribute to books. Other illustrations, however, were derived from paintings. Certain artists, such as Kawamura Bumpō and Katsushika Hokusai, spent much of their careers designing woodblock illustrations, but some painters such as Hanabusa Itchō had their works collected and published after their deaths. In either case, for the small and intimate format of the book there was a tendency to publish the most direct and evocative designs of an artist. As a result, woodblock book prints exemplify the kind of art that is akin to haiku poetry: informal, delightful, and often containing a touch of humor.

There were various purposes, beyond pure illustration, to include prints in woodblock books. One was the preservation and dissemination of earlier works of art. The oldest of the designs in this volume is the depiction of a group of horses by the great ink painter Sesson. He was following an ancient tradition of dedicating horses to Shinto shrines. Later this custom was modified to presenting pictures of horses on wooden plaques to the shrines. In 1546, Sesson completed the album of paintings of horses that were preserved and printed in woodblock form two hundred eighty years later. In this way, his symbolic gift to the shrine could be shared by the Japanese, and now also the Western, public.

Although woodblock illustrations were used in many different kinds of books, the finest artists often had their works gathered into *gafu* (picture books), and this volume illustrates some of the finest examples from *gafu* by artists of the Nanga (literati), Rimpa (decorative), and Maruyama-Shijō (naturalistic) schools. Despite the differences of style, there is a unity of feeling in these prints based upon the Japanese love for all living creatures. Artists over a period of almost four hundred years created designs that reveal their respect and their fascination with animals, birds, insects, reptiles, and fish. The woodblock book was a perfect medium for these designs, since it combines excellence of printing with intimacy of format.

The opening of Japan to the West in 1868 signaled the beginning of the end for woodblock books. Nevertheless, illustrated books continued to flourish for some decades before Western-style printing became dominant in Japan. Among the most popular artists during the later nineteenth century was Shibata Zeshin, who achieved equal fame as a painter and lacquer artist. Zeshin's *Swallow* (p. 57) is one of the few designs illustrated here that was modeled directly upon a haiku:

> From the nostril
> of the Great Buddha comes
> a swallow
>
> *Issa*

Both the poem and the woodblock print show the lively humor that informs so much Japanese art, compounded equally of surprise and delight in the natural world.

Japanese artists, like haiku poets, were at their best depicting living creatures, as these illustrations so charmingly demonstrate. Almost all of the major artists of pre-modern Japanese painting are included in woodblock books, and their achievements deserve to be better known by both scholars and the art-loving public. We hope that this volume will help to make illustrated books recognized as among the most intimate, fascinating, and enjoyable of all Japanese artistic media.

WALKERS

Evening glories—
the cat chewing the flower
has its mind elsewhere
Buson

夕がおの
花かむ猫や
よそごころ
蕪村

There's nothing
he doesn't know—
the cat on the stove
Fusei

なにもかも
知っておるなり
竈猫
風生

Between boiled barley
and romance, the female cat
has grown thin
Bashō

麦飯に
やつるる恋か
猫の妻
芭蕉

Out from the darkness
back into the darkness—
affairs of the cat
Issa

闇より
暗に入るや
猫の恋
一茶

The does
are licking each other
this frosty morning
Issa

さを鹿や
えいしてなめる
今朝の霜
一茶

Calling three times,
then no more to be heard—
the deer in the rain
Buson

三たびないて
聞こえずなりぬ
雨の鹿
蕪村

They might be gossiping
about misty days—
    horses in the field
          Issa

霞む日の
うわさするやら
  野辺の馬
     一茶

The blind horse
touched by the straw coat
    opens his mouth
       Anonymous

めくら馬
蓑がさわれば
  口を開け
     無名

Sudden evening shower—
and rising from the heat,
    the broken-down horse
        Kitō

夕立や
よみがへりたる
  たおれ馬
     几董

Lead him slowly!
the horse is carrying
    the spring moon
      Watsujin

のろく引け
馬の背中は
  春の月
     曰人

Its voice growing hoarse,
the monkey's teeth are whitened
by the moon over the peak
                                    Kikaku

声かれて
猿の歯白し
　峰の月
　　　其角

Wolves
are keening in harmony—
this snowy evening
                                    Jōsō

おおかみの
声そろうなり
　雪の暮
　　　丈草

Hiding its tail
among the ears of barley—
an old fox
                                    Tesshi

麦のほに
尾をかくさばや
　老狐
　　　轍士

A bat flies
along the rows of green willows
in the evening glow
Kikaku

青柳に
こうもりつたう
夕ばえや
其角

The bat
circling the moon
will not leave it
Gyōtai

こうもりや
月のほとりを
立ちさらず
暁台

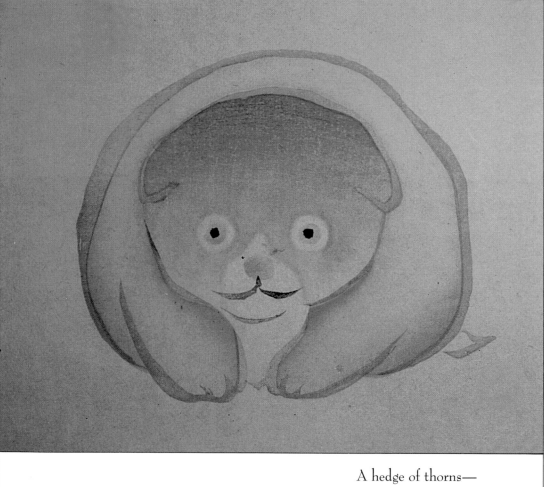

A hedge of thorns—

how skillfully the dog

wriggled under it!

Issa

茨垣

犬の上手に

もぐりけり

一茶

A single ox
in the field of flowers—
like a rock in the ocean
Anonymous

牛一つ
花野の中の
沖の石
無名

The bull's back
is thatched like a roof
in this heat
Kakō

牛の背に
屋の出来つる
暑さ哉
可幸

How beautiful—
the leanness of the cow
in the summer fields
Bonchō

うつくしく
牛のやせたる
夏野かな
凡兆

Becoming a cow
would be fine—morning naps
and the evening cool
Shikō

牛になる
合点じゃ朝ね
夕涼み
支考

Mouth open,

chasing away flies—

the watchdog

Issa

口あいて

蠅を追うなり

門の犬

一茶

The old dog

is leading the way—

visiting family graves

Issa

古犬や

先に立つなり

墓参り

一茶

In our home

the fireflies make good companions

for the mice

Issa

我宿や

鼠と仲の

よい蛍

一茶

Squeaking in response

to baby sparrows—

a nest of mice

Bashō

雀ごと

声なきかわす

鼠の巣

芭蕉

Running across the altar
and stealing a chrysanthemum—
the temple rat
Takamasa

あかだなの
菊かざしゆく
鼠かな
　高政

The pond reflects
a flying squirrel
over the wisteria
Kikaku

水影や
むささびわたる
藤の棚
　其角

Typhoons ended,
the rat swims across
the flowing waters
Buson

野分止んで
鼠のわたる
流れかな
　蕪村

Chasing a boar
through the pampas grasses—
voices of the night

Issa

しし追や、
すすきを走る
夜の声

一茶

FLIERS

As dew drips
gently, gently, the doves
murmur their chant
Issa

露ほろり
ほろりと鳩の
念仏哉
一茶

The voice of the cuckoo
slants
over the water
Bashō

ほととぎす
声横とうや
水の上
芭蕉

The cuckoo
with a single call
    has established summer
           Ryōta

時鳥
一声夏を
  さだめけり
    蓼太

The warbler
sings in the evening with
    its morning voice
          Gekkyo

鶯や
夕ぐれがたも
  朝の声
    月居

The woodpecker
has not moved at all—
    day ends
          Issa

木つつきや
一つ所に
  日の暮るる
    一茶

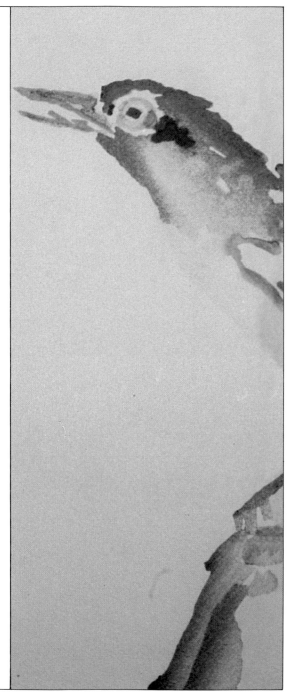

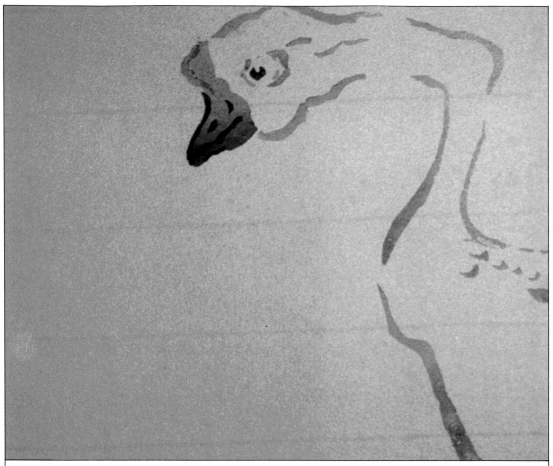

Wild geese murmuring—

are they spreading

  rumors about me?

                    Issa

雁わやわや

おれが噂を

  致すかな

          一茶

Usually detestable,
the crow, this morning,
in the snow—

Issa

日頃にくき
烏も雪の
あしたかな
一茶

Striding along
as though he were tilling the fields—
the crow

Issa

畠うちの
真似をしてあるく
烏かな
一茶

Opening his mouth to say
"this day is much too long"—
a crow

Issa

ばか長い
日やと口あく
烏かな
一茶

Give me back my dream!
a crow has wakened me
to misty moonlight

Onitsura

夢返せ
烏のさます
きりの月
鬼貫

Heads held high,

cormorants are swimming

up the swift current

Rōka

こうべたて

鵜のむれのぼる

はやせかな

浪化

The moor hen sings—

and just to its rhythm,

clouds hurry by

Issa

水鶏鳴く

ひょうしに雲が

急ぐぞよ

一茶

A floating sandal

is an object of fun

for seagulls

Anonymous

浮沓を

馬鹿にして

都鳥

無名

The warbler
wipes its muddy feet
on the plum blossoms
Issa

鶯や
泥足ぬぐう
梅の花
一茶

Competing
in the spring winds—
skylarks
Yasui

春風に
ちからくらぶる
ひばり哉
野水

Trampling on clouds,
inhaling the mist,
the skylark soars
Shiki

雲をふみ
霞をすうや
あげひばり
子規

From the nostril
of the Great Buddha comes
a swallow

Issa

大仏の

鼻からいずる

つばめ哉

一茶

The caged bird

envies the butterfly—

just look at its eyes!

Issa

かごの鳥

蝶をうらやむ

目つきかな

一茶

They have learned

to visit at mealtimes—

baby sparrows

Tayo

膳時を

おぼえて来るや

雀の子

多代

The barnyard rooster
tries to act like a lion
by preening his feathers
Kikaku

鶏の
ししに働く
逆毛かな
其角

This rooster
struts along as though
he had something to say
Anonymous

鶏の
何か言いたい
足ずかい
無名

When the eyes
of hawks are darkened—
quails call

Bashō

鷹の目も
今や暮れぬと
鳴くうずら
芭蕉

A pheasant's tail
very gently brushes
the violets

Shushiki

きじの尾の
やさしくさわる
すみれかな
秋色

A spring full of sun
on the tail of the peacock—
how it sparkles!

Meisetsu

日の春を
くじゃくの羽の
光かな
鳴雪

Owl!
Wipe that scowl off your face—
spring rain

Issa

梟よ
面癖直せ
春雨
一茶

In harmony
with the crescent moon—
the cuckoo

Issa

三日月と
そりがあうやら
ほととぎす
一茶

Even small birds
fly past and do not enter—
so deep the woods

Chine

小鳥さえ
わたるほどの
深山かな
千子

The cuckoo calls—
and the waters of the lake
cloud over a little

Jōsō

時鳥
なくや湖水の
ささ濁り
丈草

A thin layer of snow
coats the wings of mandarin ducks—
such stillness!

Shiki

おしの羽に
薄雪つもる
しずかさよ
子規

Its beauty exhausted
on a mandarin duck—
winter grove

Buson

おしどりに
美を尽くしてや
冬木立
蕪村

In the withered fields
there's no need for the crane
to stretch out its neck
Shikō

野は枯れる

のばすものなし

鶴の首

支考

If it had no voice
the heron might disappear—
this morning's snow
Chiyo

声なくば

鷺うしなわむ

今朝の雪

千代

Even herons
after six in the evening
fly two by two
Anonymous

鷺でさえ

暮六つ過は

ふたつとび

無名

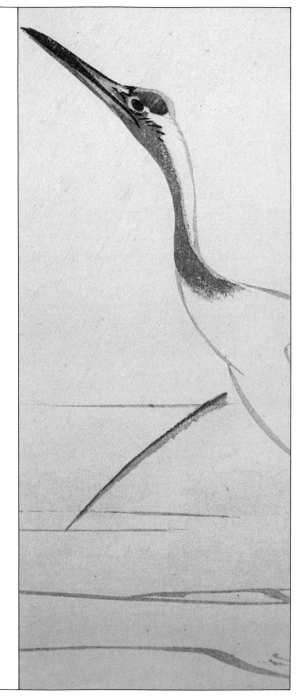

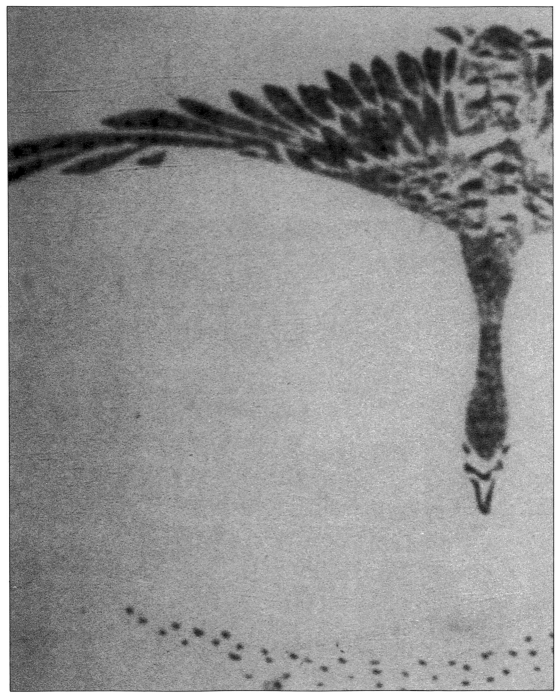

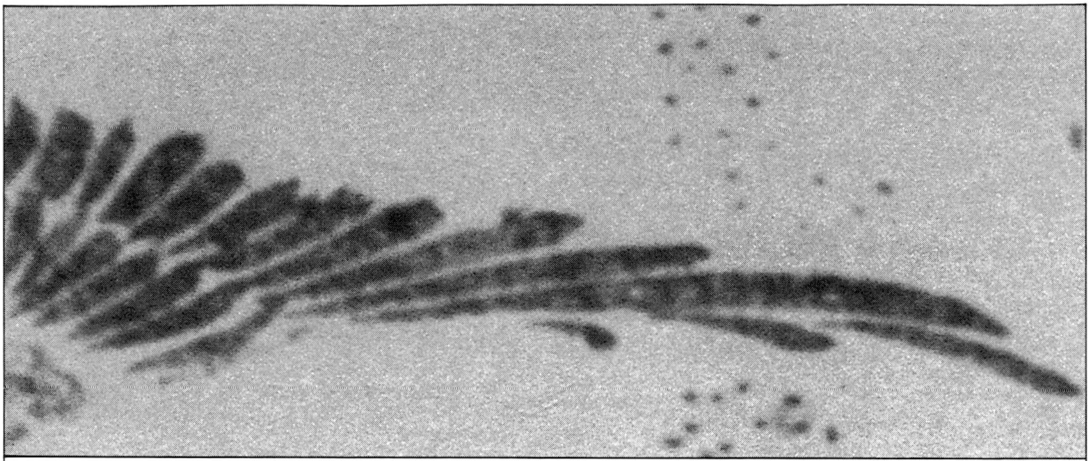

A wild goose
falling right down my neck—
frosty night
Shintoku

ぼのくぼに
雁落ちかかる
霜夜かな
信徳

An eagle blown off
the rocky crag—
early autumn gale
Ryōta

岩端の
鷲吹きはなつ
野分かな
蓼太

As the sea grows dark
the voice of the duck
faintly whitens
Bashō

海くれて
鴨の声
ほのかに白し
芭蕉

No need to cry out—
wherever you wild geese fly,
it's the same floating world
Issa

鳴くな雁
どっこも同じ
浮世ぞや
一茶

CRAWLERS

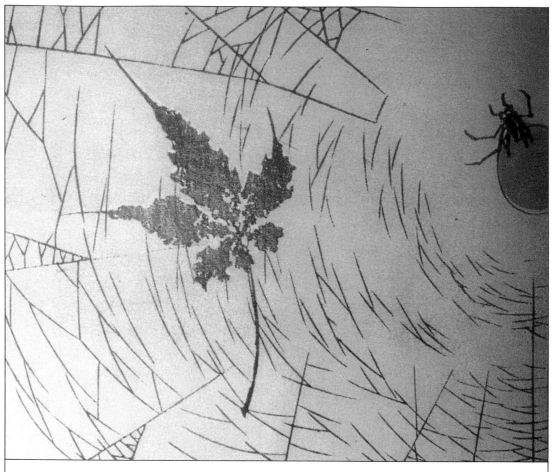

Lightning!

fleeing up the wall,

the legs of a spider

Kichō

いなずまや

壁を逃るる

蜘の足

机鳥

Down a paulownia tree

the rain comes trickling

across a cicada's belly

Baishitsu

桐の木や

雨のながるる

蟬の腹

梅室

Daybreak,
rain leaking through the roof—
the sound of insects
Gyōtai

暁や
雨もりしきり
虫の声
暁台

The cricket
proudly pricks up its whiskers
and sings
Issa

こおろぎが
髭をかつぎて
鳴きにけり
一茶

Singing as it goes,
an insect floats down the stream
on a broken bough
Issa

なきながら
むしの流るる
浮木かな
一茶

Tranquility—
the voice of the cicada
seeps into the rocks
Bashō

閑かさや
岩にしみ入る
蟬の声
芭蕉

Could they be hymns?

frogs are chanting

in the temple well

Kansetsu

釈教の

歌か寺井に

鳴く蛙

閑節

Recited on and on,

the poems of the frogs

have too many words

Eiji

長く鳴く

蛙の歌や

文字余り

永治

Bracing his feet

and offering up a song—

the frog

Sōkan

手をついて

歌申しあぐる

蛙かな

宗鑑

One after another

croak the frogs—

a poetry contest

Anonymous

たちかわり

鳴くや蛙の

歌あわせ

無名

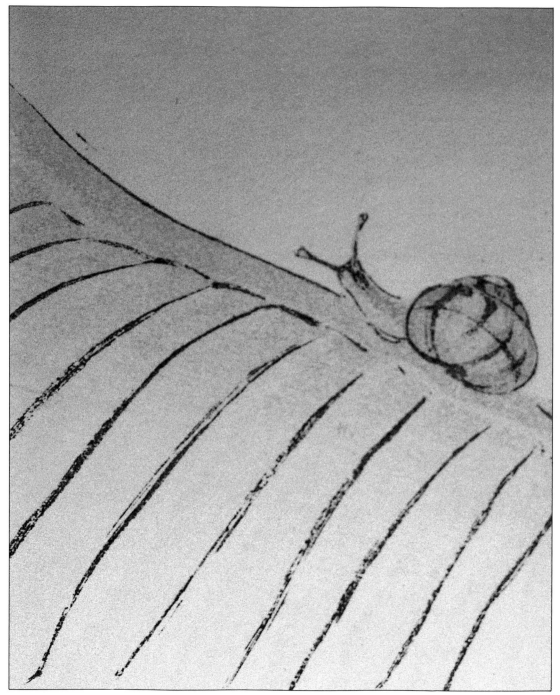

On the brushwood gate
instead of a lock—
one snail

Issa

芝の戸や
じょう代りに
かたつむり

一茶

The snail
goes to sleep and wakes up
just as he is

Issa

でで虫の
其身其まま
寝起哉

一茶

Like some of us,
he looks very important—
this snail

Issa

一ぱしの
面魂や
かたつむり

一茶

To the sounds of

horses munching grass,

fireflies dance

Issa

馬の草

食ふ音して

とぶ蛍

一茶

How curious—

running errands right and left—

fireflies

Kaiga (death poem)

面白や

左右の使いの

飛蛍

介我

Burning so easily,

extinguished so easily—

the firefly

Chine (death poem)

燃えやすく

又消えやすき

蛍かな

千子

Its light going out

just in my hand—

the firefly

(Kyōrai, when his

sister Chine died)

手の上に

かなしくきゆる

蛍かな

去来

Where there are people
there are flies, and also
there are Buddhas
Issa

人あれば
蠅あり仏
ありにけり
一茶

Don't hit me!
the fly wrings its hands
and wrings its feet
Issa

やれ打つな
蠅が手をする
足をする
一茶

They live long—
the flies, fleas, and mosquitos
in this poor village
Issa

長生の

蠅や蚤蚊や

びんぼう村

一茶

Treated with contempt
by flies and fleas—
today also comes to an end
Issa

蚤蠅に

あなどられつつ

きょうも暮れぬ

一茶

While I ponder
a snail
passes me by
Anonymous

物思ふ

向うを通る

かたつむり

無名

A grasshopper
chirps in the sleeve
of the scarecrow
Chigetsu

きりぎりす
鳴くやかがしの
袖のうち
千月

Mosquito larvae,
dancing a Buddhist chant
in the water by the grave
Issa

ぼうふらの
念仏おどりや
墓の水
一茶

Swarms of mosquitos—
but without them,
it's a little lonely
Issa

かばしらや
是もなければ
小淋しき
一茶

Withered branches—
and the evanescent memory
of a cicada's voice
Kagai (death poem)

枯枝や
はかなく残る
蟬の声

花街

Autumn—
and a cicada's husk
falls like a tear
Shiki

秋立や
ほろりと落ちし
蟬の殻

子規

Distant mountains
reflecting in its eyes—
a dragonfly
Issa

遠山が
目玉にうつる
とんぼかな
一茶

On white walls
the passing dragonflies
cast their shadows
Shōha

白壁に
とんぼ過ぐる
日影かな
召波

Dragonflies—
all facing
the setting sun
Rangai

とんぼの
向きをそろえる
西日哉
嵐外

The trail of ants
continues all the way down
from the peaks of the clouds
Issa

蟻の道
雲の峰より
つづきけん
一茶

Mountain ants
vivid
on a white peony
Buson

山ありの
あからさまなり
白ぼたん
蕪村

A butterfly
stitching together
the rows of barley
          Sora

くりかえし
麦のうねぬう
　こちょうかな
　　　曽良

Pausing for a nap
on the temple bell—
the butterfly
          Buson

釣鐘に
止りて眠る
　こちょうかな
　　　蕪村

The lizard's
triangular head—is it
getting a little longer?
          Kyoshi

三角の
とかげの顔の
　少し延ぶか
　　　虚子

Falling from a tree,
the snake slithers on the ground
in this heat
          Shikyū

木を落ちて
蛇の地を這う
　暑さかな
　　　支鳩

The snake flees—
but the eyes that peered at me
remain in the weeds
          Kyōshi

蛇にげて
我をみし目の
　草に残る
　　　虚子

Rustling, rustling,
the lotus leaves sway—
a tortoise in the pond
Onitsura

さわさわと
蓮うごかす
池の亀
鬼貫

Crouching,
peering up at the clouds—
a frog
                                    Chiyo

つくばうて
雲をうかがう
　蛙かな
　　　　千代

In perfect calm
he watches the mountain—
this frog
                                    Issa

ゆうぜんとして
山を見る
　蛙かな
　　　　一茶

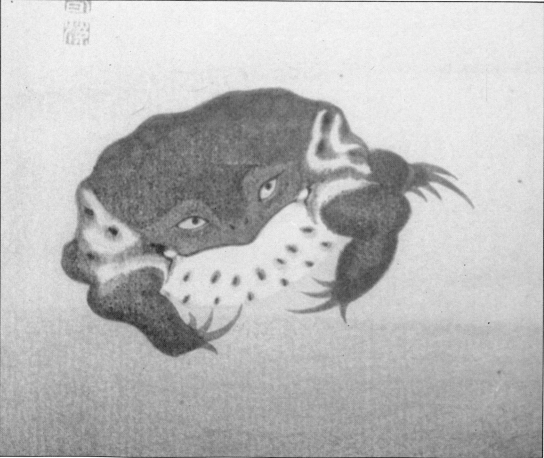

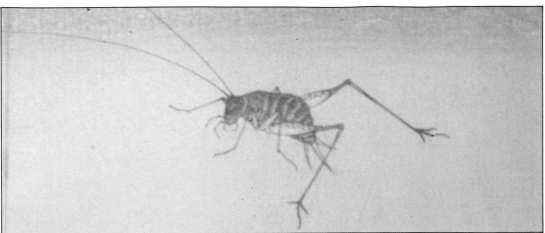

The tree frog
riding the plantain leaf
trembles
Kikaku

雨蛙
芭しょうにのりて
そよぎけり
其角

By the power
of complete non-attachment
the frog floats
Jōsō

とりつかぬ
力で浮ぶ
蛙かな
丈草

Breaking the surface
of a petal-covered pond—
frogs' eyes
Fusei

一めんの
落花の水に
蛙の目
風生

An old pond—
after jumping in,
no frog!
Bōsai

古池や
そのご飛びこむ
蛙なし
鵬斎

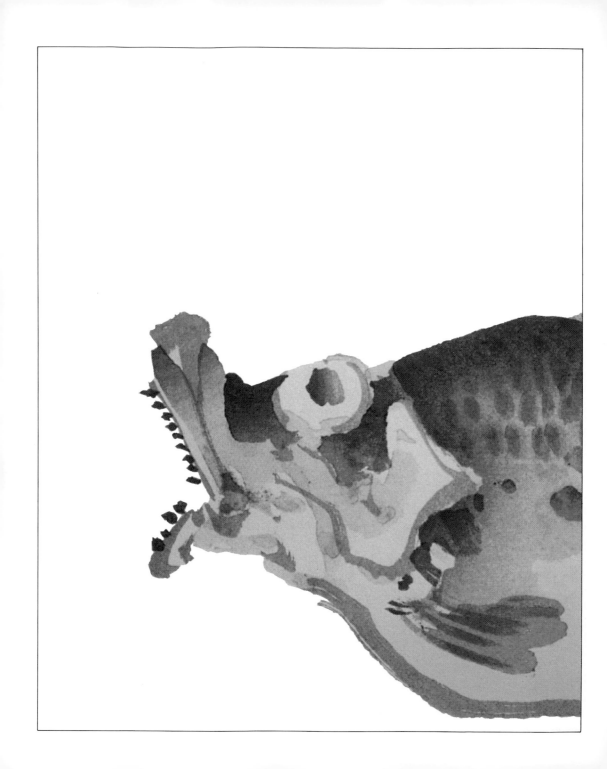

SWIMMERS

The salted seabream's
lips are also chilly—
fishmarket shelf

Bashō

しおだいの
歯茎も寒し
魚の棚

芭蕉

The fish
don't know they're in a bucket—
cooling by the gate

Issa

魚どもや
桶とも知らで
門涼み

一茶

A sudden shower
drums down upon
the heads of the carp
Shiki

夕立に
うたるる鯉の
あたまかな
子規

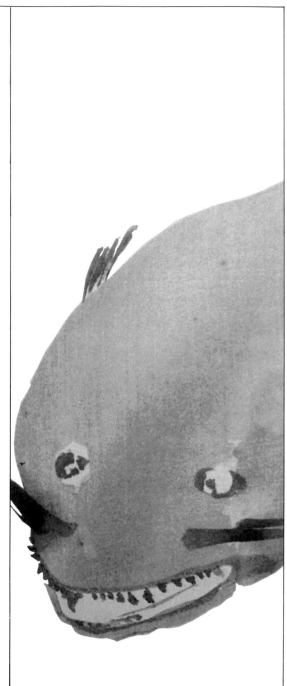

At daybreak
the whitefish whitens
just a little
Bashō

あけぼのや
しら魚白き
こと一寸
芭蕉

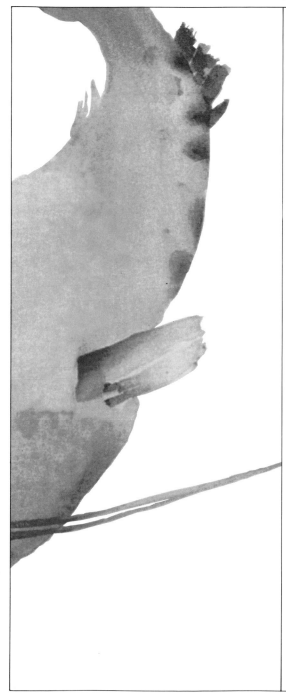

The trout leaps up—
and below him a stream of
clouds floats by
Onitsura

飛鮎の
底に雲ゆく
流れかな
鬼貫

In the pond
the fish are motionless—
autumn wind
Seisei

水中に
動かぬ魚や
秋の風
青青

Short summer night—

flowing among the rushes,

bubbles from crabs

Buson

みじか夜や

芦間流るる

蟹の泡

蕪村

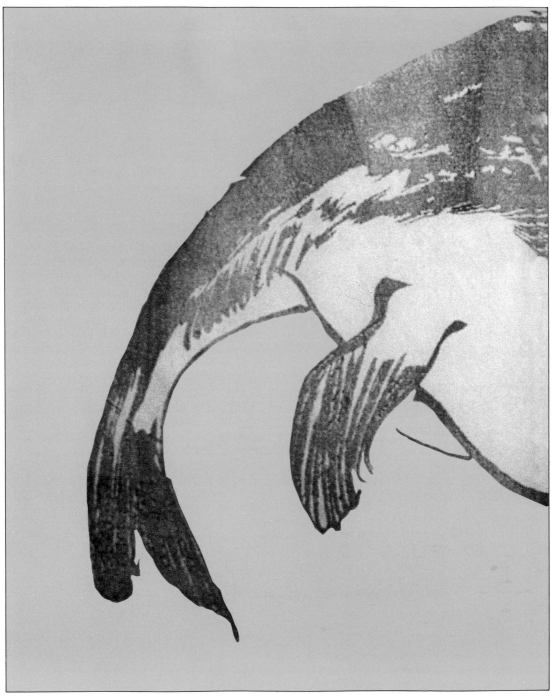

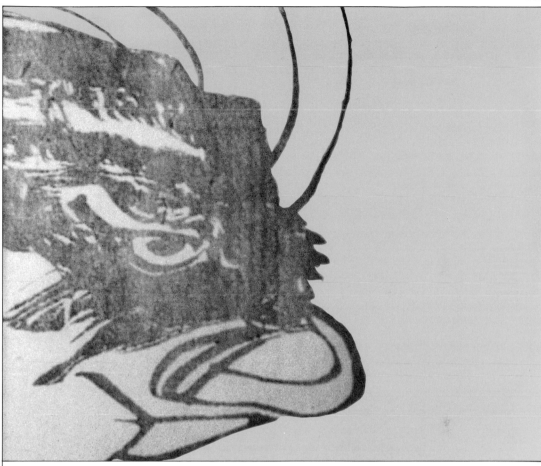

Sad stories

whispered to the jellyfish

by the seaslug

Shōha

憂きことを

海月に語る

海鼠かな

召波

Frozen together,

what are they dreaming?

seaslugs

Seisei

こおりおうて

何を夢見る

海鼠かな

青青

The clam
keeps its mouth shut—
in this heat
Bashō

蛤の
口しめている
暑さかな
芭蕉

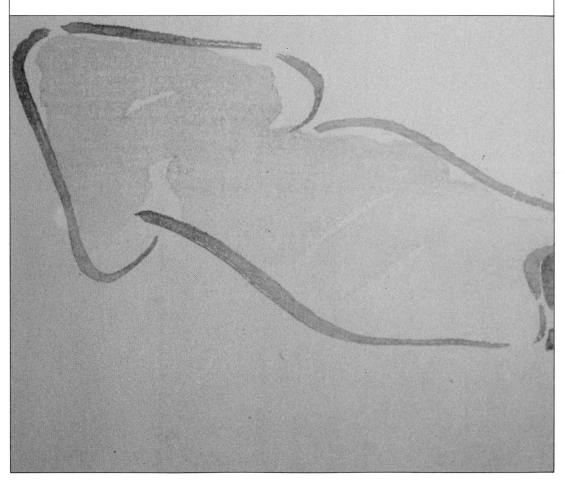

Octopus pot—
evanescent dreams
of the summer moon
Bashō

蛸壺や
はかなき夢を
夏の月
芭蕉

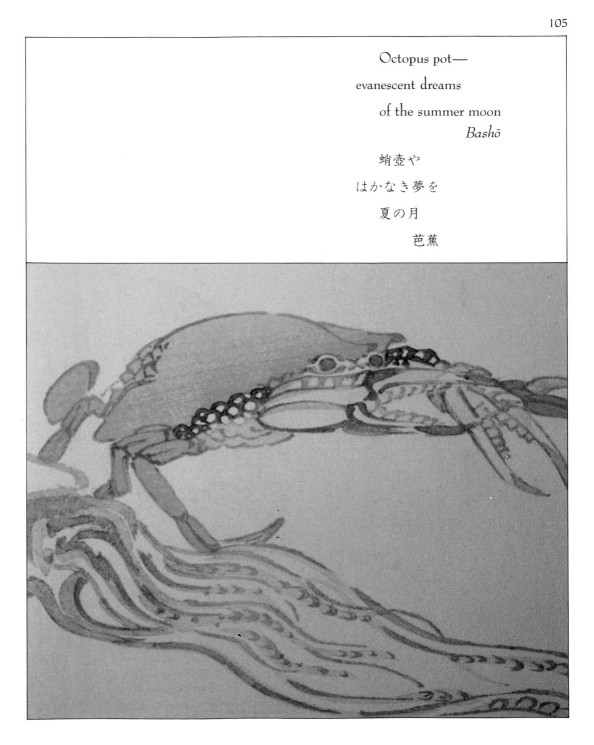

THE ARTISTS

Fusetsu Yūjō (dates unknown) Born in Bishū, Yūjō studied with Naitō Tōhō and then worked in Kyoto, painting in the Shijō style.

Hanabusa Itchō (1652–1724) Itchō was born in Osaka, the second son of a doctor. He was ordained a monk, but withdrew from Buddhist orders to become a painter. After studying with Kanō Yasunobu, Itchō was expelled from the Kanō school because of his free spirit. At one time he was exiled by the Shogunate for his parodies, but he was pardoned in 1709 and lived his final years in Edo. Itchō utilized his Kanō technique for paintings and book designs of many kinds, and was especially known for his genre scenes and his frequent use of humor. His pupils prepared a five-volume set of one hundred of his designs as the *Eihitsu Hyakuga*.

Hatta Koshū (1760–1822) Hatta Koshū was a pupil of both Maruyama Ōkyo and his son Ōzui. He was known for his paintings of bird-and-flower and figure themes.

Itō Jakuchū (1716–1800) Jakuchū was one of the great individualist painters of the eighteenth century, famous for his detailed paintings in color and his dynamic brushwork in ink. His designs for printing in "stone-rubbing" style (with the images appearing white on black) are highly valued by contemporary collectors.

Kanō Naonobu (1607–50) The younger brother of Tan'yū, Naonobu founded his own branch of the Kanō school in Edo, which grew to become one of the major official academies of painting. His dramatic portrayal of a goose in flight is one of the strongest woodblock designs by any Kanō-school artist.

Kanō Tan'yū (1602–74) The most important Edo period artist of the Kanō school, Tan'yū mastered all formats of painting, working for the shogunate and for major daimyo. Under his leadership, the Kanō tradition became the orthodox school of painting during the Edo period. After his death, a number of his paintings and sketches were reproduced in the Shūchin Gafu.

Katsuma Ryūsui (1711–96) A haiku poet, calligrapher, seal-carver, and painter, Ryūsui was part of the ukiyo-e world in Edo (Tokyo). His woodblock books such as *Blessings from the Sea* were among the first to be printed in full color.

Katsushika Hokusai (1760–1849) One of the most famous masters in the history of Japanese art, Hokusai was the most prolific designer of woodblock book illustrations in the Edo period, excelling at all subjects. His *One Hundred Views of Fuji* is considered one of the masterpieces of woodblock printing, just as his *Thirty-Six Views of Fuji* is celebrated as a series of single-sheet prints.

Kawamura Bumpō (1779–1821) A pupil of Kishi Ganku, Bumpō became a successful painter in Kyoto but was even more celebrated for his designs for many woodblock books. He is considered one of the greatest masters of book illustration, as can be seen from his fierce depiction of a *fugu* (blowfish) from one of his finest picture books.

Ki Baitei (1744–1810) After studying with the haiku poet and painter Yosa Buson, Baitei lived most of his life in Omi Province (present-day Shiga Prefecture), where he painted powerful landscapes and lively depictions of human figures. His animal paintings are rare, but he did several designs of living creatures for his woodblock masterpiece, the *Kyūrō Gafu*.

Kitagawa Utamaro (1745–1806) Although he is most famous for his single-sheet Ukiyo-e prints of beautiful women, Utamaro also designed some splendid woodblock books on various subjects including birds, shells, and insects.

Maruyama Ōzui (1766–1829) As the eldest son and pupil of Maruyama Ōkyo, Ōzui eventually became the second head of the Maruyama school. He was known for his excellent brushwork technique and refined use of line and color.

Matsumoto Hōji (dates unknown) Born in Osaka, Hōji studied with the poet-painter Yosa Buson. As an artist, Hōji became especially known for his paintings of frogs, which he endowed with largeness of scale and a certain mournful charm.

Miyamoto Kunzan (dates unknown) A Nanga artist who lived in Osaka, Kunzan is today little known, but his designs for woodblock books show his serious study of Chinese-style painting methods. His picture of a monkey also demonstrates his sly sense of humor.

Mochizuki Gyokusen (1834–1913) The third generation of painters with the same name, Gyokusen studied Maruyama-Shijō and Kishi school painting styles, then lived in Kyoto where he became celebrated for his paintings of bird-and-flower and landscape themes.

Mori Shunkei (dates unknown) A pupil of Mori Sosen, Shunkei was active in the first two decades of the nineteenth century. His woodblock book on insects is celebrated as a classic of the genre.

Mori Sosen (1747–1821) Most famous for his paintings of monkeys, Sosen founded his own "Mori" school, but is more broadly considered a master in the Shijō tradition of naturalism.

Nagayama Kōin (1765–1849) A *kyōka* poet and artist, Kōin studied Shijō-style naturalistic painting under Goshun, and later contributed designs to a number of illustrated books.

Nakabayashi Chikutō (1776–1853) As the most conservative and Sinophile of Nanga masters, Chikutō devoted his life to creating his own subtle transformations of the major Chinese literati painting styles. A more intuitive side of his nature can be seen in his woodblock books of bird-and-flower subjects.

Nakamura Hōchū (dates unknown) One of the last of the Rimpa-school masters to live and work in Kyoto, Hōchū was most celebrated for his fan paintings. He designed the *Kōrin Gafu* in honor of the great Rimpa master Ogata Kōrin.

Sesson Shūkei (1504–89?) The last of the great Muromachi-period ink painters, Sesson was a Zen monk who admired the style of Sesshū but painted in his own idiosyncratic manner. His works are characterized by their boldness of conception and strength of brushwork. His designs of horses, prepared originally for a Shinto shrine, are some of the earliest designs ever printed in woodblock-book format.

Shibata Zeshin (1807–91) Shibata Zeshin is best known for his work in lacquer, but he also became an excellent Shijō-style painter under the tutelage of Suzuki Nanrei. Zeshin produced many excellent designs for woodblock books, the earliest of which is illustrated here.

Suzuki Mannen (1868–93) The third son of the Shijō-school painter Suzuki Hyakunen, Mannen died at the age of twenty-six, just when his own career as an artist was beginning to attract attention in his native Kyoto.

Tachibana Morikuni (1679–1748) Born in Osaka, Morikuni studied under a pupil of Kanō Tan'yū. However, he was expelled from the Kanō school because in one of his books he published some designs that were considered to be secret teachings of the Kanō tradition. His pictures of animals demonstrate the liveliness of his artistic spirit.

Tanaka Nikka (died 1845) A pupil of Toyohiko, Nikka was an artist of the Shijō school in Kyoto. He was considered especially talented at painting flowers, animals, and birds.

Tani Bunchō (1763–1840) Although usually classified as a Nanga (literati) painter, Bunchō actually worked in a great many different styles. He was one of the most successful artists in Edo (Tokyo) during the early nineteenth century, and his work appears in many woodblock books.

Tsubaki Chinzan (1801–54) One of the leading pupils of Watanabe Kazan, Chinzan excelled at bird-and-flower themes, often painting without outlines in the "boneless" tradition to achieve a soft and vibrant effect. He also could display a sense of humor, as in his depiction of a goose from the *Chinzan Gafu*.

Watanabe Kazan (1793–1841) Originally a pupil of Tani Bunchō, Kazan became one of the major late Edo-period Nanga masters. He is also revered as a cultural hero because he was imprisoned by the Shogunate for advocating reforms; he committed suicide while under arrest. As an artist, Kazan is difficult to classify because he excelled at many subjects, including portraits. He was equally adept at portraying a rooster, a redfish, and a singing bird in his *Kazan Gafu*.

THE POETS

Baishitsu (1769–1852)　Baishitsu was born in Kanazawa to a family of sword experts. He moved to Kyoto, visited Edo for twelve years, and then settled again in Kyoto where he became one of the major haiku teachers of his era.

Bashō (1644–94)　The most famous haiku poet in Japanese history, in his teens Bashō served Tōdō Yoshitada as a samurai retainer. His master Yoshitada studied haiku with Kitamura Sogin and called himself Sengin. During his Period, Bashō began to study haiku. When Sengin died at the age of twenty-five, Bashō left samurai life. His deep humanity, intense observation of the natural world, and depth of spirit combined to elevate the haiku tradition to its epitome.

Bonchō (died 1714)　By profession a doctor, Bonchō edited a famous book of haiku poems with Kyōrai, and also wrote many fresh and original haiku of his own. He was also interested in European studies, and was imprisoned for trading illegally with Dutch merchants.

Bōsai (1752–1826)　One of the leading Confucian scholars and Chinese-style poet-calligraphers of his day, Bōsai only rarely wrote haiku. He inscribed his verse about "the old pond" over a portrait of Bashō.

Buson (1716–83)　Around the age of seventeen, Buson went to Edo and studied painting and haiku. After his haiku teacher's death in 1742, Buson wandered around the eastern provinces for more than ten years, later settling in Kyoto. Buson is now considered one of the greatest artists in the literati style, and second only to

Bashō in the haiku tradition. Buson's verses as well as his paintings show the warmth and brilliance of his vision of humanity and the natural world.

Chigetsu (1634?–1708?)　Chigetsu, the wife of a freight agent, studied haiku with Bashō, and became one of the four famous women poets of her era. After the death of her husband in 1686, she became a nun. She lived in Ōtsu with her son Otokuni, who also studied with Bashō and became a fine haiku poet.

Chine (?–1688?)　Chine was the younger sister of Kyōrai, who was one of the ten leading pupils of Bashō. On her early twenties, Chine and Kyōrai traveled together to Ise. During this trip, Chine wrote haiku poems which were considered as good as or even better than those by her older brother.

Chiyo (1703–75)　One of the most famous women poets, Chiyoni started writing haiku on her own at the age of fifteen. She also studied with Shikō, and became a nun shortly after she reached the age of fifty. Her poems were popular because of her simple and witty mastery of everyday language.

Eiji (dates unknown)

Fusei (1885–1979)　Fusei traveled in Europe and the United States, then returned to Japan to study under Kyōshi. Eventually he became one of the leading haiku poets of the early twentieth century.

Gekkyo (1756–1824)　Born in Kyoto, Gekkyo along with Kitō became one of the leading pupils of Buson. Upon Buson's death, Gekkyo established his own school and became known as one of the three major haiku poets of his era, the two others being Suzuki Michihiko of Edo and Inoue Shirō of Nagoya.

Gyōtai (1732–92) A native of Nagoya, Gyōtai tried to elevate haiku from the vulgarity of his day and return to the excellence of Bashō. He also followed the lead of Buson in creating poems combining strength of imagery with keen observation of the world around him.

Issa (1762–1826) Issa had a difficult life. The eldest son of a poor farmer, he was soon orphaned, and later in life his wives and several children died before him. Issa wrote poems with such compassion for all living creatures that he became (with Bashō and Buson) one of the three most loved poets in the haiku tradition. Issa was especially sensitive to insects, which are usually ignored or scorned in the literature of the Western world.

Jōsō (1662–1704) Because of poor health, Jōsō gave up his life as a samurai at the age of twenty-six and entered the priesthood. He studied haiku with Bashō, and after the death of his master, Jōsō lived a solitary life. His poems are considered to express lonely feelings most effectively.

Kagai (died 1778)

Kaiga (1652–1718) A pupil of Bashō, Kaiga was a close friend of the poet Kikaku.

Kakō (dates unknown)

Kansetsu (dates unknown)

Kichō (dates unknown) Kichō was best known as a critic and evaluator of poetry competitions.

Kikaku (1661–1707) One of the ten chief disciples of Bashō, Kikaku studied medicine with Kusakari San'etsu, Confucianism with Hattori Kansai, Chinese-style poetry with the Enkakuji priest Daiten, calligraphy with Sasaki Genryū, and painting with Hanabusa Itchō, who is also represented in this book. Kikaku's poems are sophisticated and often have touches of wit and humor.

Kitō (1741–89) Learning haiku first from his father Kikei, and later from Buson, Kitō also greatly admired the poems of Kikaku. Kitō wrote haiku with direct and unsentimental observations. He loved sakè, and like several other haiku poets he became a monk in his final years.

Kyōrai (1651–1704) Born in Nagasaki, Kyōrai moved to Kyoto at the age of eight and became known for his excellence in martial arts, astronomy, and general learning. He met Kikaku in 1684 and joined him to become one of the ten leading pupils of Bashō. He combined in his own verse the qualities of martial strength and poetic gentleness. Kyōrai's writings about poetics became influential for later haiku masters.

Kyōshi (1874–1959) Kyōshi was one of the masters of the haiku tradition in the late Meiji, Taishō, and early Shōwa periods. The name Kyōshi was given him by Masaoka Shiki. Kyōshi inherited Shiki's haiku magazine *Hototogisu* and continued Shiki's literary circle, where writers and poets reviewed their own work. Kyōshi also wrote novels and essays, but was most celebrated for his poems which were traditional in style but fresh in spirit.

Meisetsu (1847–1926) Born in Tokyo, Meisetsu studied Chinese literature in his youth and did not turn to haiku until he was forty-six years old, under the influence of Shiki. He achieved great fame for his poetry during the late Meiji and Taishō eras.

Moritake (1473–1549) Born in an Ise Shinto priest's family, Moritake served as a Shinto priest at the Ise shrine. Together with Sōkan, he developed a new form of *renga* from which poems could be excerpted as haiku.

Onitsura (1661–1738) At the age of eight, Onitsura began to learn haiku. At thirteen, he became a pupil of Matsue Shigeyori, and he also received instructions from Kitamura Kigin and Nishiyama Sōin. In 1865, Onitsura stated that he came to realize that sincerity was the most important quality in poetry. Thus, his haiku poems were written in a simple and straightforward style.

Rangai (1758–1831) Rangai was a pupil of Rankō and Gyōtai in haiku, and became known as a painter as well as a poet.

Rōka (1671–1703) Rōka, the son of the abbot of Higashi Honganji in Kyoto, became the eleventh chief priest of Zuisenji Temple in Toyama at the age of seven. He came to know Kyōrai, and in 1694 Rōka became a pupil of Bashō and studied haiku with him. Rōka's haiku are known for their clarity and strength of observation.

Ryōta (1718–87) Ryōta, who settled in Edo in his youth, studied with Rito, who was a pupil of Ransetsu. Ryōta later became famous as a haiku poet and teacher with more than three thousand pupils.

Seisei (1869–1937) A poet from Osaka, Seisei was a follower of Shiki and wrote haiku in traditional style, opposing radical change in the world of poetry. In 1902, he became the haiku editor of the Asahi Newspaper.

Shigeyori (1602–80) Born in Matsue, Shigeyori lived most of his life in Kyoto. He studied *renga* with Satomura Shōtaku and haiku with Matsunaga Teitoku. Later, because of a conflict with Ryuho, another pupil of Teitoku, Shigeyori left his teacher. He taught such fine poets as Onitsura and Gonsui. Shigeyori also compiled the first book of Bashō's haiku.

Shiki (1867–1902) Despite the brevity of his life, Shiki became the most influential haiku poet and theorist of the last century. He first studied Chinese literature and calligraphy, then after a hemorrhage of the lungs, turned to politics, philosophy, and aesthetics. Finally he took up haiku, advocating a return to the poetic ideals of Buson. Shiki's own poems show his keen observation of nature and display great sensitivity.

Shikō (1665–1731) After serving as a Zen monk at Daichiji, Shikō became a doctor, later meeting and becoming a disciple of Bashō. When told he might be reborn as an animal if he did not lead a pure life, Shikō observed that it might well be an improvement.

Shikyū (dates unknown)

Shintoku (1633–98) Born in Kyoto, Shintoku traveled widely on his business as a wealthy merchant. He followed several different early haiku traditions and distinguished himself as a poet whose haiku showed crisp and sensitive observation of nature.

Shōha (died 1771) Shōha studied Chinese poems with Hattori Nankaku. A beloved haiku pupil of Buson, Shōha died before his teacher, and Buson thereupon wrote a preface for Shōha's collected haiku that became very famous. Shōha's own poems show his keen visual sense.

Shūshiki (1669–1725?) Shūshiki studied with Kikaku, and she married the haiku poet Kangyoku, also a pupil of Kikaku. Shūshiki's poems became famous for their gentle and humane observations of everyday life.

Sobaku (1758–1821) A pupil of Gyōtai, Sobaku was an admirer of Bashō's pupil Sora and a friend of the haiku poet Shirō. Sobaku gave up his life as a merchant to become a poet-priest, and he became very skilled at haiku poem-painting.

Sōkan (1458?–1546?) From a samurai family, Sōkan served the shogun Ashikaga Yoshihisa. After his father's death, however, Sōkan became a monk and lived the rest of his life in a hermitage, where he developed a new form of simplified *renga* poetry. In time he became considered the inventor of haiku.

Sora (1649–1710) Giving up his life as a samurai, Sora went to Edo and studied Shinto and *waka* with Kikkawa Koretaru. Later, Sora became a pupil of Bashō and often traveled with his teacher on haiku journeys.

Takamasa (dates unknown) A follower of the Kyoto Danrin school of haiku, Takamasa lived in Kyoto and befriended pupils of Teitoku. He wrote haiku poems describing natural scenes in an unpretentious, free, and sometimes wild style.

Tayo (1776–1865) A haiku pupil of doctor and poet Michihiko (1757–1819), Tayo moved to Edo in 1823, where she lived as a haiku master until the age of ninety. Her two sons also became good haiku poets.

Tesshi (died 1707) Tesshi traveled widely in the Kansai, Kanto, and northern areas of Japan. The book by Tesshi entitled *Hanamiguruma* is a collection of gossip about haiku poets who appear in the book as courtesans.

Watsujin (1758–1836) A poet in the Gyōtai tradition, Watsujin was a samurai from Sendai who wrote haiku under a variety of art names.

Yasui (1658–1743) A merchant from Nagoya, Yasui was a pupil Bashō and wrote many haiku following the Bashō tradition. After his wife died, his interests gradually shifted to *waka* and the tea ceremony.

THE ILLUSTRATIONS

WALKERS

pp. 18–19 Mori Sosen, *Meika Gafu* (A Book of Pictures by Celebrated Artists, 1814), Monkey

p. 21 Hanabusa Itchō, *Eihitsu Hyakuga* (One Hundred Brush Drawings by Itchō, 1773), Cat

p. 22 Nagayama Kōin, *Meika Gafu* (1814), Deer

p. 25 Sesson Shūkei, *Gagaku Sōsho* (A Series of Drawing Studies, 1826), Horses. Spencer Collection, New York Public Library

p. 26 Miyamoto Kunzan, *Kanga Hitori Geiko* (Practicing Chinese-style Drawings by Oneself, 1807), Monkey

pp. 28–29 Tsubaki Chinzan, *Chinzan Gafu* (A Book of Pictures by Chinzan, 1880), Bat. Spencer Collection, New York Public Library

pp. 30–31 Nakamura Hōchū, *Korin Gafu* (A Book of Pictures by Kōrin, 1802), Puppies. Spencer Collection, New York Public Library

p. 33 Tanaka Nikka, *Kyūhōdō Gafu* (A Book of Pictures by Kyūhōdō [Nikka], 1856), Ox. Spencer Collection, New York Public Library

pp. 34–35 Hatta Koshū, *Koshū Gafu* (A Book of Pictures by Koshū, 1812), Dog. Spencer Collection, New York Public Library

p. 37 Mochizuki Gyokusen, *Gyokusen Shūgajō* (An Album of Studies by Gyokusen, 1891), Mouse

p. 38 Kanō Tan'yu, *Shūchin Gafu* (A Rare Collection of Paintings, 1801), Squirrels

pp. 40–41 Tachibana Morikuni, *Ehon Shahobukuro* (A Picture Book of Sketching Treasures, 1720), Boar

FLIERS

pp. 42–43 Kanō Tan'yu, *Shūchin Gafu* (1801), Rooster and Hen

pp. 44–45 Watanabe Kazan, *Kazan Gafu* (A Book of Pictures by Kazan, 1907), Dove. Spencer Collection, New York Public Library

pp. 46–47 Watanabe Kazan, *Kazan Gafu* (1907), Songbird. Spencer Collection, New York Public Library

pp. 48–49 Tsubaki Chinzan, *Chinzan Gafu* (1880), Goose. Spencer Collection, New York Public Library

p. 51 Ki Baitei, *Kyūrō Gafu* (A Book of Pictures by Kyūrō [Baitei], 1799), Crow.

p. 52 Hanabusa Itchō, *Eihitsu Hyakuga* (1773), Cormorant

p. 54 Maruyama Ōzui, *Meika Gafu* (1814), Songbird.

p. 57 Shibata Zeshin, *Shoga Kaisui* (A Selection of Calligraphy and Painting, 1832), Swallow

pp. 58–59 Watanabe Kazan, *Kazan Gafu* (1907), Rooster. Spencer Collection, New York Public Library

The "Weathermark" identifies this book as a production of Weatherhill, publishers of fine books on Asia and the Pacific. Editorial supervision: Jeffrey Hunter. Book design and typography by Liz Trovato. Typesetting by Trufont, Hicksville, New York. Printing and binding by Oceanic Graphic Printing. The typefaces used are Bernhard Modern for the text and Tiepolo Book for the display type.